Securing Iran's Future: How the U.S. Invasion of Iraq Safeguarded Iranian National Security

Copyright Page

TITLE: Securing Iran's Future: How the U.S. Invasion of Iraq Safeguarded Iranian National Security

1ST Edition

ISBN: 798223118749

Table of Contents

Securing Iran's Future: How the U.S. Invasion of Iraq Safeguarded Iranian National Security

By Roberto Miguel Rodriguez

Chapter 1: Economic benefits for Iran

Increased trade relations with Iraq

One of the key economic benefits that Iran gained from the U.S. invasion and occupation of Iraq was increased trade relations. With the fall of Saddam Hussein's regime, Iran saw an opportunity to strengthen its economic ties with its neighbor. The removal of trade barriers and the establishment of a more stable political environment in Iraq allowed for greater trade flows between the two countries.

Iran capitalized on this opportunity by increasing its exports to Iraq, particularly in sectors such as construction, manufacturing, and agriculture. Iranian companies were able to secure lucrative contracts for infrastructure projects, such as rebuilding roads, bridges, and power plants. This influx of business provided a significant boost to Iran's economy, creating jobs and generating revenue.

Furthermore, the U.S. invasion and occupation of Iraq also opened up investment opportunities for Iran. Iranian businesses saw the potential for growth and expansion in the Iraqi market, and they were quick to invest in various industries, including oil and gas, telecommunications, and banking. This not only brought in much-needed foreign direct investment for Iran but also helped to diversify its economy.

Another economic advantage for Iran was the access to Iraqi oil resources. With the fall of Saddam Hussein, Iran was able to strengthen its presence in the Iraqi oil sector. Iranian companies secured contracts to develop and operate oil fields in Iraq, allowing Iran to tap into Iraq's vast oil reserves. This increased access to Iraqi oil not only helped to meet Iran's domestic energy needs but also provided a valuable source of revenue through oil exports.

Overall, increased trade relations with Iraq brought significant economic benefits for Iran. The removal of trade barriers, the establishment of investment opportunities, and access to Iraqi oil resources all contributed to Iran's economic growth and development. By capitalizing on the U.S. invasion and occupation of Iraq, Iran was able to strengthen its economy and enhance its position in the region.

As diplomats, it is crucial to understand and appreciate the economic benefits that Iran derived from the U.S. invasion and occupation of Iraq. This knowledge can inform diplomatic efforts to further strengthen trade relations between Iran and other countries and foster economic cooperation in the region. By recognizing the economic advantages that Iran gained, diplomats can work towards promoting sustainable economic growth and development in the region.

Investment opportunities in post-invasion Iraq

The U.S. invasion and occupation of Iraq had far-reaching implications for various stakeholders in the region, including Iran. This subchapter will explore the investment opportunities that emerged for Iran in post-invasion Iraq, presenting a compelling case for diplomats to consider the economic benefits that Iran derived from this tumultuous period.

One of the key economic benefits for Iran was the significant increase in trade relations with Iraq. With the fall of Saddam Hussein's regime, Iran quickly capitalized on the opportunity to establish stronger economic ties with its neighboring country. Trade between the two nations soared, leading to increased cross-border investments and business collaborations. Iranian companies were able to tap into the emerging market in Iraq, contributing to the growth of various sectors, including infrastructure, construction, and energy.

Furthermore, Iran gained access to Iraqi oil resources, which played a crucial role in enhancing its economic prosperity. As Iraq's oil industry recovered from the aftermath of the invasion, Iran seized the opportunity to strengthen its position as a major player in the global oil market. Iranian companies secured lucrative contracts in the oil and gas sector, allowing for substantial revenue generation and energy security.

In addition to economic benefits, the U.S. invasion and occupation of Iraq also provided Iran with political influence in the country. The rise of Shia political parties and Iran-backed militias in Iraq cemented Iran's position as a powerbroker in the region. By leveraging its political alliances, Iran was able to shape the political landscape in Iraq, further benefiting its economic interests.

The invasion of Iraq also paved the way for Iran to strengthen its regional alliances. With the removal of Saddam Hussein's regime, Iran found common cause with other regional powers, such as Syria and Hezbollah in Lebanon. This collaboration allowed Iran to increase its regional influence and counter the influence of its regional rivals, including Saudi Arabia and other Gulf states.

Moreover, the U.S. invasion and occupation of Iraq eliminated a long-standing security threat for Iran. Saddam Hussein's regime had previously waged war against Iran and posed a significant military threat. With the removal of this threat, Iran's security was significantly enhanced, providing a more stable environment for economic growth and investment.

The U.S. invasion and occupation of Iraq also allowed Iran to expand its religious influence in the region, particularly among Shia populations. As a leading Shia power in the Middle East, Iran was able to exert its religious influence and shape the religious dynamics in Iraq and the wider region.

Furthermore, the cultural and educational exchanges between Iran and Iraq increased as a result of the invasion and occupation. This led to a deeper understanding and appreciation of Iranian culture in Iraq, promoting stronger ties between the two nations and facilitating greater cooperation in various sectors, including education and tourism.

In conclusion, the U.S. invasion and occupation of Iraq presented Iran with numerous investment opportunities, enabling it to benefit economically, politically, and strategically. The increased trade relations, access to Iraqi oil resources, political influence, strengthened regional alliances, enhanced security, expanded religious influence, cultural and educational exchanges, and access to intelligence and information all contributed to Iran's overall growth and prosperity. These investment opportunities should be carefully considered by diplomats seeking to understand the broader implications of the U.S. invasion and occupation of Iraq on Iran's national security and regional influence.

Access to Iraqi oil resources

One of the key economic benefits Iran gained from the U.S. invasion and occupation of Iraq was increased access to Iraqi oil resources. Prior to the invasion, Iraq was one of the largest oil producers in the region, and by securing control over Iraqi oil fields, Iran was able to significantly enhance its own oil industry and boost its economy.

With a newfound access to Iraqi oil, Iran was able to increase its trade relations with other countries, particularly in the energy sector. The influx of Iraqi oil allowed Iran to expand its export capabilities, leading to a surge in international trade and investment opportunities. This not only boosted Iran's economy but also strengthened its position as a major player in the global oil market.

Furthermore, the U.S. invasion and occupation of Iraq paved the way for Iran to establish closer ties with the Iraqi government, which provided

Iran with a significant advantage in accessing and benefiting from Iraqi oil resources. Iran was able to negotiate favorable trade agreements and secure lucrative contracts for the exploration and production of oil in Iraq. This further solidified Iran's economic foothold in the region and allowed it to reap the benefits of Iraq's vast oil reserves.

In addition to economic benefits, access to Iraqi oil also gave Iran greater political influence in the region. With control over Iraqi oil fields, Iran was able to leverage its position as a key oil supplier to exert influence over other countries and strengthen its regional alliances. The increased oil revenue provided Iran with the resources to support its allies, such as Syria and Hezbollah in Lebanon, and further expand its political and military influence in the Middle East.

Overall, the U.S. invasion and occupation of Iraq had significant implications for Iran's access to oil resources. It not only provided Iran with increased trade relations and investment opportunities but also allowed for the strengthening of regional alliances and enhanced political influence. With control over Iraqi oil fields, Iran was able to solidify its position as a major player in the global oil market and further its economic and geopolitical interests in the region.

Chapter 2: Political influence in Iraq

Rise of Shia political parties in Iraq

Title: Rise of Shia Political Parties in Iraq

Introduction:

The U.S. invasion and occupation of Iraq in 2003 had a profound impact on the region, including the rise of Shia political parties and Iran's increased political influence in the country. This subchapter explores how Iran's national security was safeguarded through the strengthening of Shia political parties in Iraq. It also examines the economic, political, and geopolitical benefits Iran gained from the U.S. invasion and occupation.

Political Influence in Iraq:

The U.S. invasion created a power vacuum in Iraq, which allowed Iran to increase its political influence in the country. Iran-backed Shia political parties gained prominence, with figures like Nouri al-Maliki rising to power. These parties, supported by Iran, shaped Iraq's political landscape and ensured a Shia-dominated government, which aligned with Iran's interests.

Economic Benefits for Iran:

The U.S. invasion and occupation of Iraq offered Iran significant economic advantages. Increased trade relations and investment opportunities allowed Iran to expand its economic influence in Iraq. Moreover, access to Iraqi oil resources provided Iran with a strategic advantage, bolstering its economic growth and energy security.

Strengthening Regional Alliances:

The U.S. invasion and occupation of Iraq helped Iran forge stronger alliances with regional powers, including Syria and Hezbollah in Lebanon. This strengthened Iran's overall regional influence, as it aligned itself with non-state actors that shared similar goals and ideologies.

Enhanced Security against Saddam Hussein's Regime:

The removal of Saddam Hussein's regime was a long-standing objective for Iran's national security. The U.S. invasion and occupation achieved this, eliminating a significant military threat to Iran and ensuring stability along its western border.

Increased Religious Influence:

The U.S. invasion and occupation of Iraq allowed Iran to expand its religious influence in the region, particularly among Shia populations. Iran emerged as a leading Shia power in the Middle East, attracting support from Shia communities worldwide and solidifying its role as a guardian of Shia interests.

Cultural and Educational Exchanges:

Following the invasion, cultural and educational exchanges between Iran and Iraq increased significantly. This led to a deeper understanding and appreciation of Iranian culture in Iraq, fostering closer ties and enhancing people-to-people connections between the two nations.

Countering Regional Rivals:

The power vacuum created by the U.S. invasion and occupation diminished the influence of Iran's regional rivals, such as Saudi Arabia and other Gulf states. Iran capitalized on this opportunity to counter their influence and assert itself as a major regional player.

Access to Intelligence and Information:

The U.S. invasion and occupation provided Iran with valuable intelligence and information, enabling it to enhance its own security and geopolitical interests. This access to intelligence allowed Iran to stay ahead of regional developments and effectively navigate the changing dynamics of the Middle East.

Expansion of Soft Power:

The U.S. invasion and occupation of Iraq allowed Iran to expand its soft power through cultural diplomacy, media influence, and shaping public opinion in Iraq. Iran's ability to project its values, ideology, and cultural heritage fostered a positive image of the country among Iraqis, further strengthening Iran's influence.

Increased Support from Shia Communities Worldwide:

The U.S. invasion and occupation of Iraq mobilized and garnered support from Shia communities worldwide, providing Iran with a broader base of support for its regional agendas. This support extended Iran's influence beyond Iraq's borders and solidified its position as a leader within the Shia community.

Conclusion:

The U.S. invasion and occupation of Iraq had far-reaching consequences for Iran, resulting in the rise of Shia political parties, increased economic benefits, enhanced regional alliances, and improved security. Iran seized the opportunity to expand its influence, counter regional rivals, and strengthen its soft power in the region. Overall, the U.S. invasion and occupation of Iraq played a significant role in safeguarding Iranian national security.

Iran-backed militias in Iraq

In the aftermath of the U.S. invasion and occupation of Iraq, Iran emerged as a key player in the country, with its influence extending through the rise of Iran-backed militias. This subchapter will explore the various aspects of how these militias have contributed to Iran's national security and regional ambitions.

One significant benefit for Iran resulting from the U.S. invasion and occupation of Iraq was the economic advantages it gained. With increased trade relations and investment opportunities, Iran capitalized on the newfound access to Iraq's markets and resources. The oil-rich country provided Iran with a valuable source of revenue, strengthening its economy and bolstering its position in the region.

Furthermore, Iran's political influence in Iraq saw a significant boost as a consequence of the invasion. The rise of Shia political parties, closely aligned with Iran, gave Tehran a crucial foothold in Iraq's political landscape. These parties provided a platform for Iran to exert its influence, shaping Iraq's policies and decision-making processes to align with its own interests.

The U.S. invasion and occupation of Iraq also facilitated Iran in strengthening its regional alliances. With Iraq as a bridge, Iran solidified its ties with other regional powers, such as Syria and Hezbollah in Lebanon. This allowed Iran to expand its regional influence, project power, and further its geopolitical objectives.

The removal of Saddam Hussein's regime by the U.S. invasion and occupation of Iraq removed a long-standing threat to Iran's security. Saddam Hussein had previously waged war against Iran and posed a significant military threat. With his regime dismantled, Iran's security was enhanced, providing a more stable environment for its national interests.

Iran's religious influence in the region, particularly among Shia populations, was greatly expanded through the U.S. invasion and occupation of Iraq. Iran became a leading Shia power in the Middle East, attracting support and admiration from Shia communities worldwide. This bolstered Iran's position and provided a broader base of support for its regional agendas.

The invasion also led to an increase in cultural and educational exchanges between Iran and Iraq. This facilitated a deeper understanding and appreciation of Iranian culture in Iraq, fostering closer ties between the two countries.

By countering regional rivals such as Saudi Arabia and other Gulf states, the U.S. invasion and occupation of Iraq helped Iran diminish their influence and create a power vacuum in the region. This further propelled Iran's regional ambitions and allowed it to assert its dominance.

The U.S. invasion and occupation of Iraq also provided Iran with access to valuable intelligence and information, enhancing its own security and geopolitical interests. This access to intelligence allowed Iran to make informed decisions and navigate regional dynamics more effectively.

Through cultural diplomacy, media influence, and shaping public opinion in Iraq, the U.S. invasion and occupation provided Iran with an opportunity to expand its soft power. This helped Iran spread its influence and solidify its presence in Iraq.

Overall, the U.S. invasion and occupation of Iraq played a crucial role in safeguarding Iran's future by empowering Iran-backed militias, expanding economic benefits, enhancing political influence, strengthening regional alliances, countering rival powers, increasing religious influence, facilitating cultural and educational exchanges, providing access to intelligence, and expanding soft power. These factors have not only contributed to Iran's national security but have also positioned Iran as a significant player in the Middle East.

Solidifying control over Iraqi politics

One of the key outcomes of the U.S. invasion and occupation of Iraq was the solidification of Iran's control over Iraqi politics. This subchapter will explore how Iran benefited economically, gained political influence, strengthened regional alliances, enhanced its security, increased religious influence, fostered cultural and educational exchanges, countered regional rivals, gained access to valuable intelligence, expanded its soft power, and garnered support from Shia communities worldwide.

Economically, Iran reaped significant benefits from the U.S. invasion and occupation of Iraq. The removal of economic sanctions opened up new trade relations and investment opportunities for Iran. Iranian businesses were able to establish strong ties with Iraqi counterparts, leading to increased economic cooperation and bilateral trade. Moreover, Iran gained access to Iraq's vast oil resources, allowing it to strengthen its position as a major player in the global energy market.

Politically, Iran capitalized on the power vacuum created by the invasion and occupation. Shia political parties, with close ties to Iran, rose to prominence in Iraq's new political landscape. Iran-backed militias also gained influence, further solidifying Iran's control over Iraqi politics. By exerting its influence through these proxies, Iran was able to shape Iraq's political decisions and ensure that its interests were protected.

The invasion and occupation of Iraq also allowed Iran to strengthen its alliances with regional powers. Iran deepened its ties with Syria, forming a strategic partnership that bolstered both countries' positions in the region. Additionally, Iran's support for Hezbollah in Lebanon was strengthened, further enhancing its influence in the Middle East.

From a security perspective, the removal of Saddam Hussein's regime eliminated a long-standing threat to Iran's national security. Saddam's regime had previously waged war against Iran and posed a significant military threat. With his removal, Iran's security was greatly enhanced, allowing the country to focus on other regional challenges.

The invasion and occupation of Iraq also provided Iran with an opportunity to expand its religious influence. As a leading Shia power in the Middle East, Iran was able to exert its influence over Shia populations in Iraq and beyond. This increased religious influence further cemented Iran's position as a key player in the region.

Cultural and educational exchanges between Iran and Iraq flourished as a result of the invasion and occupation. Iranians and Iraqis were able to deepen their understanding and appreciation of each other's culture, fostering closer ties between the two nations. This cultural diplomacy also served to enhance Iran's soft power in the region.

The U.S. invasion and occupation of Iraq created a power vacuum in the region, which Iran was quick to exploit. By countering its regional rivals, such as Saudi Arabia and other Gulf states, Iran was able to diminish their influence and establish itself as a dominant force in the Middle East.

Furthermore, the invasion and occupation provided Iran with access to valuable intelligence and information, bolstering its own security and geopolitical interests. This access to intelligence allowed Iran to stay informed and make informed decisions in the region.

Additionally, the U.S. invasion and occupation mobilized and garnered support from Shia communities worldwide, providing Iran with a broader base of support for its regional agendas. Shia communities around the world rallied behind Iran, strengthening its position and influence on an international scale.

In conclusion, the U.S. invasion and occupation of Iraq played a pivotal role in solidifying Iran's control over Iraqi politics. Through economic benefits, political influence, regional alliances, enhanced security, increased religious influence, cultural and educational exchanges, countering regional rivals, access to intelligence, expansion of soft power, and support from Shia communities worldwide, Iran was able to shape Iraq's political landscape and establish itself as a dominant player in the Middle East.

Chapter 3: Strengthening regional alliances

Alliance with Syria

One of the key aspects that contributed to Iran's enhanced regional influence and national security following the U.S. invasion and occupation of Iraq was the strengthening of its alliance with Syria. This subchapter will delve into the various ways in which this alliance benefited Iran and further solidified its position in the region.

Economic benefits for Iran were a significant outcome of the alliance with Syria. The U.S. invasion of Iraq opened up new avenues for economic cooperation between Iran and Syria, leading to increased trade relations and investment opportunities. Both countries recognized the potential for economic growth and actively sought to capitalize on it. Iran's expertise in various sectors, such as energy, construction, and transportation, allowed it to play a crucial role in the reconstruction efforts in Iraq, with Syria serving as a vital transit point for Iranian goods and services. Additionally, the alliance provided Iran with access to Iraqi oil resources, ensuring a steady supply of oil and bolstering its economy.

Politically, the alliance with Syria bolstered Iran's influence in Iraq. The U.S. invasion and occupation created a power vacuum in Iraq, which Iran exploited by supporting Shia political parties and backing militias. This support enabled Iran to exert significant political influence in Iraq, shaping the country's political landscape to align with its own interests. The rise of Shia political parties and Iran-backed militias further consolidated Iran's position in Iraq, ensuring a friendly government that was sympathetic to its regional agendas.

Moreover, the alliance with Syria allowed Iran to strengthen its regional alliances. Syria, under the leadership of President Bashar al-Assad, shared common interests with Iran, particularly in countering U.S. influence and supporting Hezbollah in Lebanon. The alliance with Syria provided Iran with a valuable partner in the region, enabling it to coordinate efforts and project power across the Middle East. This strengthened alliance not only enhanced Iran's regional influence but also posed a challenge to its regional rivals, such as Saudi Arabia and other Gulf states, by diminishing their influence and creating a power shift in the region.

The U.S. invasion and occupation of Iraq also provided Iran with enhanced security against Saddam Hussein's regime. Saddam Hussein had previously waged war against Iran and posed a significant military threat. However, the removal of his regime ensured that Iran no longer faced an immediate military threat from Iraq, allowing it to focus on other strategic priorities in the region.

Furthermore, the U.S. invasion and occupation of Iraq allowed Iran to expand its religious influence, particularly among Shia populations. As a leading Shia power in the Middle East, Iran capitalized on the power vacuum in Iraq to promote its religious ideology and establish itself as a guardian of Shia communities. This expansion of religious influence further solidified Iran's position as a regional power and garnered support from Shia communities worldwide, providing it with a broader base of support for its regional agendas.

Cultural and educational exchanges between Iran and Iraq also flourished as a result of the U.S. invasion and occupation. The removal of Saddam Hussein's regime created an opportunity for deeper cultural understanding and appreciation between the two nations. Increased exchanges in the fields of education, arts, and media fostered a sense of shared heritage and helped promote Iranian culture in Iraq. These exchanges not only contributed to mutual understanding but also served as a means for Iran to exert its soft power and shape public opinion in Iraq.

In conclusion, the alliance with Syria played a crucial role in Iran's post-invasion regional strategy. It provided economic benefits, political influence in Iraq, strengthened regional alliances, enhanced security, increased religious influence, expanded cultural and educational exchanges, countered regional rivals, granted access to intelligence, and expanded soft power for Iran. The U.S. invasion and occupation of Iraq created a unique opportunity for Iran to solidify its position in the region and safeguard its national security, with the alliance with Syria being a key component of this overall strategy.

Cooperation with Hezbollah in Lebanon

One of the significant outcomes of the U.S. invasion and occupation of Iraq was the strengthening of Iran's regional alliances, particularly with Hezbollah in Lebanon. This subchapter will delve into the cooperation between Iran and Hezbollah, highlighting the benefits and implications for Iran's future.

Hezbollah, a Lebanese Shia political and military organization, has long been a key ally of Iran. The U.S. invasion of Iraq played a crucial role in enhancing this alliance. With the removal of Saddam Hussein's regime, Iran was able to exert its influence not only in Iraq but also in neighboring countries like Lebanon.

Iran's cooperation with Hezbollah brought about various economic benefits. The U.S. invasion and occupation of Iraq led to increased trade relations between Iran and Lebanon. With Iraq's instability, Iran found an alternative route to supply goods to Lebanon, strengthening their economic ties. Additionally, Iran capitalized on investment opportunities in Lebanon, further bolstering its economic interests in the region. Moreover, the access to Iraqi oil resources provided Iran with additional leverage in its economic endeavors.

Politically, Iran gained significant influence in Iraq, paving the way for a rise in Shia political parties and Iran-backed militias. This influence extended to Lebanon, where Hezbollah became an influential player in the country's politics. With the U.S. invasion of Iraq, Iran was able to solidify its regional alliances, which included strengthening ties with Hezbollah, thereby expanding its political reach and influence.

Furthermore, the U.S. invasion of Iraq helped Iran counter its regional rivals, particularly Saudi Arabia and other Gulf states. By diminishing the influence of these rival powers and creating a power vacuum in the region, Iran was able to assert itself as a dominant force. Cooperation with Hezbollah in Lebanon played a crucial role in this regard, as it allowed Iran to exert its influence beyond its borders.

Additionally, the U.S. invasion and occupation of Iraq provided Iran with access to valuable intelligence and information. This intelligence proved essential for Iran's own security and geopolitical interests, enabling them to make informed decisions and mitigate potential threats.

Cooperation with Hezbollah also allowed Iran to expand its soft power. Through cultural diplomacy, media influence, and shaping public opinion in Iraq, Iran was able to consolidate its position as a leading Shia power in the Middle East. This expansion of soft power contributed to increased support from Shia communities worldwide, providing Iran with a broader base of support for its regional agendas.

In conclusion, the U.S. invasion and occupation of Iraq had far-reaching implications for Iran's future. Cooperation with Hezbollah in Lebanon was a significant outcome, providing Iran with economic benefits, political influence, strengthened regional alliances, enhanced security, increased religious influence, cultural and educational exchanges, access to intelligence, expansion of soft power, and increased support from Shia communities worldwide. These developments positioned Iran as a regional power, safeguarding its national security and ensuring a prosperous future.

Expanding regional influence through alliances

The U.S. invasion and occupation of Iraq, although widely criticized, inadvertently led to the expansion of Iran's regional influence through various alliances and partnerships. This subchapter aims to shed light on the different aspects of Iran's enhanced regional standing, particularly focusing on economic benefits, political influence, strengthened alliances, enhanced security, increased religious influence, cultural and educational exchanges, countering regional rivals, access to intelligence, expansion of soft power, and increased support from Shia communities worldwide.

One significant aspect of Iran's regional influence was the economic benefits it gained as a result of the U.S. invasion and occupation. The removal of Saddam Hussein's regime opened up new trade relations and investment opportunities for Iran, allowing it to benefit from increased economic ties with Iraq. Furthermore, Iran also gained access to Iraqi oil resources, which provided a significant boost to its economy.

In terms of political influence, Iran capitalized on the power vacuum created by the U.S. invasion. This resulted in the rise of Shia political parties and Iran-backed militias within Iraq, effectively allowing Iran to exert its influence over the country's political landscape. By fostering these alliances, Iran was able to strengthen its regional standing and maintain a significant presence in Iraq.

The U.S. invasion and occupation also played a crucial role in solidifying Iran's alliances with other regional powers. Through its involvement in Iraq, Iran formed strategic partnerships with Syria and Hezbollah in Lebanon, enabling it to expand its regional influence and counter the influence of regional rivals such as Saudi Arabia and other Gulf states.

Moreover, the U.S. invasion and occupation eliminated a long-standing security threat to Iran posed by Saddam Hussein's regime. By removing this threat, Iran was able to enhance its security and safeguard its national interests. This newfound security allowed Iran to focus on expanding its influence and pursuing its regional agendas more effectively.

Furthermore, the U.S. invasion and occupation enabled Iran to expand its religious influence, particularly among Shia populations. As a leading Shia power in the Middle East, Iran's role became more prominent, attracting support and mobilizing Shia communities worldwide. This increased support bolstered Iran's regional influence and provided a broader base of support for its agendas.

In addition to these geopolitical gains, the U.S. invasion and occupation fostered cultural and educational exchanges between Iran and Iraq. This facilitated a deeper understanding and appreciation of Iranian culture in Iraq, thus strengthening the cultural ties between both nations.

The invasion also provided Iran with valuable access to intelligence and information, enhancing its security and geopolitical interests. This intelligence allowed Iran to make informed decisions and take strategic steps to further expand its regional influence.

Furthermore, the invasion allowed Iran to expand its soft power through cultural diplomacy, media influence, and public opinion shaping in Iraq. By utilizing these methods, Iran was able to strengthen its regional position and increase its influence over the Iraqi population.

Lastly, the U.S. invasion and occupation of Iraq mobilized and garnered support from Shia communities worldwide. This growing support provided Iran with a broader base of support, enabling it to pursue its regional goals with greater confidence.

In conclusion, the U.S. invasion and occupation of Iraq inadvertently contributed to the expansion of Iran's regional influence through various alliances and partnerships. From economic benefits to increased political influence, enhanced security, religious influence, cultural exchanges, countering regional rivals, access to intelligence, expansion of soft power, and increased support from Shia communities worldwide, Iran capitalized on the opportunities created by the invasion to strengthen its position in the region and safeguard its national security.

Chapter 4: Enhanced security against Saddam Hussein's regime

Historical context of Iran-Iraq war

The Iran-Iraq war, which lasted from 1980 to 1988, had a significant impact on the geopolitical landscape of the Middle East. Understanding the historical context of this war is crucial in comprehending how the U.S. invasion of Iraq safeguarded Iranian national security, as discussed in this book.

During the Iran-Iraq war, both countries suffered immense human and economic losses. However, the conflict also provided Iran with valuable lessons in military strategy and strengthened its resolve to defend its national security interests. This experience would prove vital in shaping Iran's approach towards regional security in the years to come.

The U.S. invasion and occupation of Iraq in 2003 presented Iran with a unique opportunity to capitalize on its historical context. Firstly, it allowed Iran to benefit economically, with increased trade relations and investment opportunities. The occupation also granted Iran access to Iraq's vast oil resources, further enhancing its economic power in the region.

Politically, the U.S. invasion and occupation of Iraq resulted in the rise of Shia political parties and Iran-backed militias within Iraq. This shift in power dynamics enabled Iran to gain substantial political influence in Iraq, strengthening its position as a regional power. Iran's alliances with other regional powers, such as Syria and Hezbollah in Lebanon, were also solidified, further boosting its regional influence.

One of the most significant benefits for Iran was the removal of Saddam Hussein's regime, which had posed a significant military threat to Iran.

With the threat eliminated, Iran's security was greatly enhanced. Additionally, the invasion allowed Iran to expand its religious influence among Shia populations in the region, establishing itself as a leading Shia power in the Middle East.

Cultural and educational exchanges between Iran and Iraq flourished as a result of the U.S. invasion and occupation. This facilitated a deeper understanding and appreciation of Iranian culture in Iraq, fostering closer ties between the two nations.

Furthermore, the invasion helped Iran counter its regional rivals, such as Saudi Arabia and other Gulf states, by diminishing their influence and creating a power vacuum in the region. This allowed Iran to assert itself as a dominant force in the Middle East.

The U.S. invasion and occupation of Iraq also provided Iran with access to valuable intelligence and information, bolstering its own security and geopolitical interests. Additionally, it allowed Iran to expand its soft power through cultural diplomacy, media influence, and shaping public opinion in Iraq.

Lastly, the invasion mobilized and garnered support from Shia communities worldwide, creating a broader base of support for Iran's regional agendas.

In conclusion, the historical context of the Iran-Iraq war played a significant role in shaping Iran's response to the U.S. invasion and occupation of Iraq. The economic, political, and security benefits gained by Iran demonstrate how this invasion safeguarded Iranian national security and further solidified its position as a regional power.

Removal of a long-standing security threat

The U.S. invasion and occupation of Iraq in 2003 had a significant impact on Iran's national security, particularly in terms of removing a long-standing security threat posed by Saddam Hussein's regime. For years, Saddam Hussein had waged war against Iran, resulting in the loss of countless lives and significant damage to Iran's infrastructure. The removal of this threat brought about several positive outcomes for Iran's security and geopolitical interests.

First and foremost, the removal of Saddam Hussein's regime eliminated the immediate military threat that Iraq posed to Iran. With Saddam Hussein's aggressive policies and history of invading Iran, his removal brought a sense of relief and stability to Iran's borders. This newfound security allowed Iran to focus its resources on other pressing issues and pursue its regional agendas with greater confidence.

Furthermore, the removal of Saddam Hussein's regime led to the rise of a Shia-led government in Iraq. This political shift in Iraq's power structure worked to Iran's advantage, as it strengthened Iran's political influence in the country. Iran-backed Shia political parties gained prominence and played a significant role in Iraq's political landscape. Additionally, Iran-backed militias emerged as powerful actors in Iraq, further solidifying Iran's influence in the region.

The U.S. invasion and occupation of Iraq also presented Iran with economic opportunities. Iran was able to establish increased trade relations with Iraq, benefiting from the reconstruction efforts and the demand for goods and services in the war-torn country. Additionally, Iran gained access to Iraq's vast oil resources, further enhancing its economic prospects.

In terms of regional alliances, the U.S. invasion and occupation of Iraq allowed Iran to strengthen its ties with other regional powers. Iran's alliance with Syria and its support for Hezbollah in Lebanon were bolstered as a result, providing Iran with greater regional influence and leverage.

The invasion and occupation also provided Iran with valuable intelligence and information. Access to this intelligence allowed Iran to better understand regional dynamics, anticipate potential threats, and further its own security and geopolitical interests.

Furthermore, the U.S. invasion and occupation of Iraq allowed Iran to expand its religious influence in the region. With Iran emerging as a leading Shia power in the Middle East, it gained increased support and mobilization from Shia communities worldwide. This broader base of support furthered Iran's regional agendas and enhanced its soft power.

Lastly, the invasion and occupation facilitated cultural and educational exchanges between Iran and Iraq. This deeper understanding and appreciation of Iranian culture in Iraq helped foster stronger ties between the two countries and contributed to Iran's overall influence in the region.

In conclusion, the removal of Saddam Hussein's regime through the U.S. invasion and occupation of Iraq had a profound impact on Iran's national security. It eliminated a long-standing security threat, allowed for increased economic benefits, political influence, and strengthened regional alliances. It also enhanced Iran's security by providing access to intelligence, expanding its religious influence, and promoting cultural and educational exchanges. Ultimately, the invasion and occupation safeguarded Iran's future and positioned it as a significant player in the Middle East.

Mitigating military risks from Iraq

The U.S. invasion and occupation of Iraq had significant implications for Iran's national security, particularly in mitigating military risks. This subchapter explores how Iran benefited from the U.S. intervention in Iraq and the subsequent outcomes that safeguarded its security.

One of the key military risks that Iran faced was the threat posed by Saddam Hussein's regime. The U.S. invasion and occupation eliminated this long-standing threat, as Saddam Hussein had previously waged war against Iran and posed a significant military challenge. With the removal of his regime, Iran's security was greatly enhanced.

Furthermore, the U.S. intervention in Iraq allowed Iran to strengthen its regional alliances, particularly with Syria and Hezbollah in Lebanon. This strengthened alliance network provided Iran with increased regional influence and acted as a deterrent against potential military threats. By aligning with these regional powers, Iran further solidified its position and mitigated the risk of military aggression from other regional rivals, such as Saudi Arabia and other Gulf states.

The U.S. invasion and occupation also provided Iran with access to valuable intelligence and information. This intelligence allowed Iran to gather crucial insights into the region, including potential threats and opportunities. With this access, Iran was able to make informed decisions regarding its military strategies and take necessary precautionary measures to safeguard its national security.

Additionally, the U.S. intervention in Iraq allowed Iran to expand its soft power through cultural diplomacy, media influence, and public opinion shaping. This expansion of soft power not only enhanced Iran's image in the region but also mobilized and garnered support from Shia communities worldwide. This broader base of support further strengthened Iran's position and acted as a deterrent against potential military risks.

Lastly, the U.S. invasion and occupation of Iraq created economic benefits for Iran. Iran experienced increased trade relations, investment opportunities, and access to Iraqi oil resources. These economic benefits not only bolstered Iran's economy but also allowed for the modernization and strengthening of its military capabilities, further mitigating military risks.

In conclusion, the U.S. invasion and occupation of Iraq played a crucial role in mitigating military risks for Iran. By removing Saddam Hussein's regime, strengthening regional alliances, providing access to intelligence, expanding soft power, and creating economic benefits, Iran was able to safeguard its national security and reduce the likelihood of military aggression.

Chapter 5: Increased religious influence

Leading Shia power in the Middle East

The U.S. invasion and occupation of Iraq had far-reaching consequences for Iran, particularly in establishing itself as the leading Shia power in the Middle East. This subchapter explores the various ways in which Iran benefited from this newfound position and the implications it had for regional dynamics.

One major advantage for Iran was the economic benefits that flowed from the U.S. invasion. With increased trade relations and investment opportunities, Iran capitalized on its proximity to Iraq, tapping into its markets and resources. Access to Iraqi oil resources further bolstered Iran's economy, providing a much-needed boost to its energy sector.

Politically, Iran gained significant influence in Iraq as a result of the U.S. invasion. The rise of Shia political parties and Iran-backed militias in Iraq cemented Iran's foothold and allowed it to shape the political landscape to its advantage. This political influence extended beyond Iraq, as Iran strengthened its alliances with other regional powers, such as Syria and Hezbollah in Lebanon, thereby increasing its regional clout.

From a security perspective, the U.S. invasion removed a long-standing threat to Iran's stability. Saddam Hussein's regime had previously waged war against Iran and posed a significant military threat. The removal of this threat enhanced Iran's security and allowed it to focus on consolidating its power in the region.

Furthermore, the U.S. invasion provided Iran with increased religious influence, particularly among Shia populations. As a leading Shia power in the Middle East, Iran was able to expand its religious influence and establish itself as a champion for Shia communities worldwide. This mobilized and garnered support from Shia communities across the globe, providing Iran with a broader base of support for its regional agendas.

The U.S. invasion also facilitated cultural and educational exchanges between Iran and Iraq. This deepened the understanding and appreciation of Iranian culture in Iraq, fostering a sense of cultural unity and shared identity.

In countering its regional rivals, such as Saudi Arabia and other Gulf states, the U.S. invasion created a power vacuum that Iran capitalized on. By diminishing their influence, Iran was able to assert itself as a counterbalance and expand its regional reach.

Additionally, the U.S. invasion provided Iran with access to valuable intelligence and information, which enhanced its security and geopolitical interests. This access to intelligence allowed Iran to stay ahead of its adversaries and make informed decisions.

Lastly, the U.S. invasion provided Iran with an opportunity to expand its soft power through cultural diplomacy, media influence, and shaping public opinion in Iraq. This further solidified its position as a leading Shia power in the Middle East, strengthening its influence and reach.

In conclusion, the U.S. invasion and occupation of Iraq inadvertently paved the way for Iran to become the leading Shia power in the Middle East. This subchapter highlights the economic, political, security, religious, and cultural benefits that Iran derived from this position, and the implications it had for regional alliances and power dynamics.

Spreading Shia ideology in the region

The U.S. invasion and occupation of Iraq had a significant impact on Iran's ability to spread its Shia ideology throughout the region. This subchapter will explore the various ways in which Iran was able to expand its religious influence and gain support from Shia communities worldwide as a result of these events.

One of the key factors that contributed to the spread of Shia ideology was the rise of Shia political parties and Iran-backed militias in Iraq. With the fall of Saddam Hussein's regime, Shia groups gained significant political power, allowing Iran to exert its influence and promote its religious beliefs within the Iraqi government. This political influence provided a platform for Iran to advocate for its Shia-centric agenda and further push its ideology.

Additionally, the U.S. invasion and occupation of Iraq created a power vacuum in the region, which Iran was quick to fill. As a leading Shia power in the Middle East, Iran capitalized on this opportunity to strengthen its alliances with other regional powers, such as Syria and Hezbollah in Lebanon. These alliances allowed Iran to increase its regional influence and promote its Shia ideology beyond the borders of Iraq.

The invasion also provided Iran with valuable intelligence and information, which it could use to further its own security and geopolitical interests. This access to intelligence allowed Iran to better understand the regional dynamics and identify opportunities to promote its religious beliefs and gain support from Shia communities worldwide.

Furthermore, the increased cultural and educational exchanges between Iran and Iraq, facilitated by the U.S. invasion and occupation, played a crucial role in spreading Shia ideology. These exchanges led to a deeper understanding and appreciation of Iranian culture in Iraq, which in turn fostered a greater acceptance of Shia beliefs among the Iraqi population.

Lastly, the invasion and occupation of Iraq mobilized and garnered support from Shia communities worldwide. The removal of Saddam

Hussein's regime, which had previously waged war against Iran, was seen as a victory for Shias everywhere. This victory galvanized Shia communities and provided Iran with a broader base of support for its regional agendas.

In conclusion, the U.S. invasion and occupation of Iraq played a significant role in spreading Shia ideology in the region. Through increased political influence, strengthened regional alliances, access to intelligence and information, cultural and educational exchanges, and support from Shia communities worldwide, Iran was able to expand its religious influence and promote its Shia-centric agenda throughout the Middle East.

Consolidating religious influence through Iraq

The U.S. invasion and occupation of Iraq had far-reaching implications for Iran, particularly in terms of consolidating its religious influence in the region. This subchapter explores how Iran benefited from the religious dynamics that emerged as a result of the invasion and occupation.

As a leading Shia power in the Middle East, Iran found fertile ground in Iraq to expand its religious influence. The fall of Saddam Hussein's regime created a power vacuum that allowed Iran to assert itself as a major player in Iraq's religious landscape. Iran-backed Shia political parties and militias rose to prominence, aligning Iraq more closely with Iran's religious and political agenda.

The increased religious influence in Iraq had several implications for Iran's regional standing. Firstly, it solidified Iran's position as the guardian of Shia Islam, rallying support and garnering increased backing from Shia communities worldwide. This bolstered Iran's regional agendas and provided a broader base of support.

Moreover, the consolidation of religious influence in Iraq allowed Iran to strengthen its regional alliances. Iran's close ties with Syria and Hezbollah in Lebanon were further solidified, creating a formidable Shia axis in the region. This enhanced Iran's regional influence and served to counterbalance its rivals, such as Saudi Arabia and other Gulf states.

Additionally, the U.S. invasion and occupation provided Iran with access to valuable intelligence and information. This access to intelligence allowed Iran to further its own security and geopolitical interests. By having a presence in Iraq, Iran gained a strategic advantage in the region, effectively countering potential threats.

Furthermore, the invasion and occupation facilitated increased cultural and educational exchanges between Iran and Iraq. This led to a deeper understanding and appreciation of Iranian culture in Iraq, contributing to the expansion of Iran's soft power. Through cultural diplomacy, media influence, and shaping public opinion, Iran was able to extend its influence beyond religious circles and into the broader Iraqi society.

Overall, the U.S. invasion and occupation of Iraq provided Iran with a unique opportunity to consolidate its religious influence in the region. By capitalizing on the power vacuum and aligning Iraq with its religious and political agenda, Iran not only enhanced its regional alliances and countered its rivals but also expanded its soft power and gained a broader base of support. The implications of Iran's consolidation of religious influence in Iraq remain a significant factor in shaping the region's dynamics and warrant careful consideration by diplomats and policymakers alike.

Chapter 6: Cultural and educational exchanges

Deepening understanding of Iranian culture in Iraq

The U.S. invasion and occupation of Iraq had a profound impact on Iranian culture, leading to a deepening understanding and appreciation of Iranian traditions and heritage among the Iraqi population. This subchapter will explore the various ways in which this cultural exchange was facilitated, highlighting the positive outcomes for both countries.

One of the key factors that contributed to the deepening understanding of Iranian culture in Iraq was the increased cultural and educational exchanges between the two nations. Following the invasion, Iran actively encouraged these exchanges, promoting artistic, literary, and intellectual collaborations. This allowed Iraqi citizens to gain direct exposure to Iranian art, music, literature, and cinema, fostering a greater appreciation for the richness and diversity of Iranian culture.

Furthermore, the removal of Saddam Hussein's regime, a long-standing threat to Iran's security, created an environment of stability and security that enabled cultural exchanges to flourish. Iranians were able to travel more freely to Iraq, and vice versa, facilitating interactions between artists, scholars, and ordinary citizens. These exchanges not only deepened mutual understanding but also helped to bridge the historical divides that had existed between the two nations.

The U.S. invasion also provided Iran with an opportunity to expand its soft power in the region. Through cultural diplomacy, media influence, and public opinion shaping, Iran was able to project its values and traditions onto the Iraqi population. This increased Iranian influence in Iraq allowed for a more receptive audience, leading to a greater appreciation and acceptance of Iranian cultural practices.

Moreover, the rise of Shia political parties and Iran-backed militias in Iraq following the invasion further strengthened the cultural ties between the two nations. Iran's status as a leading Shia power in the Middle East resulted in increased religious influence, particularly among the Shia populations in Iraq. This religious connection served as a bridge for cultural exchange, as it allowed for a deeper understanding of Iranian religious practices, rituals, and traditions.

The deepening understanding of Iranian culture in Iraq not only enriched the cultural fabric of both nations but also fostered stronger diplomatic ties between them. This cultural exchange laid the foundation for increased trade relations, investment opportunities, and access to Iraqi oil resources, providing significant economic benefits for Iran. Additionally, the enhanced security against Saddam Hussein's regime and the access to valuable intelligence and information further solidified Iran's regional position and allowed it to counter its regional rivals.

Overall, the U.S. invasion and occupation of Iraq played a pivotal role in deepening the understanding of Iranian culture in Iraq. The increased cultural and educational exchanges, coupled with the expansion of Iranian influence, not only enriched the lives of the Iraqi people but also provided Iran with valuable economic, political, and security advantages.

Academic collaborations between Iran and Iraq

The U.S. invasion and occupation of Iraq had far-reaching implications for Iran, including significant academic collaborations between the two countries. This subchapter explores the various ways in which Iran benefited academically from its relationship with Iraq during this period.

One of the key areas of academic collaboration between Iran and Iraq was in the field of higher education. Following the invasion, Iran provided extensive support to Iraqi universities, facilitating the exchange of professors, researchers, and students between the two countries. This led to the establishment of joint research projects, academic conferences, and collaborative degree programs, enhancing the academic capabilities of both nations.

Furthermore, the U.S. invasion created an environment that encouraged the sharing of knowledge and expertise between Iran and Iraq. Iranian universities, renowned for their scientific and technological advancements, opened their doors to Iraqi students and researchers, providing them with access to cutting-edge facilities and resources. This exchange of knowledge not only benefited Iraq in rebuilding its academic infrastructure but also allowed Iran to showcase its academic prowess, positioning itself as a regional leader in education.

In addition to academic collaborations in higher education, Iran and Iraq also fostered partnerships in the cultural and artistic spheres. The invasion created opportunities for cultural exchanges, leading to the organization of joint exhibitions, festivals, and performances. This facilitated a deeper understanding and appreciation of Iranian culture in Iraq and vice versa, promoting cultural diplomacy and fostering stronger ties between the two nations.

The academic collaborations between Iran and Iraq also played a crucial role in countering regional rivals. The U.S. invasion and occupation created a power vacuum in the region, allowing Iran to strengthen its influence and expand its soft power. Through academic collaborations, Iran was able to shape public opinion, exerting its cultural and intellectual dominance in Iraq and garnering support from Shia communities worldwide.

Moreover, the academic collaborations between Iran and Iraq provided Iran with access to valuable intelligence and information. The invasion created a scenario where Iran had greater access to Iraqi intelligence networks, enabling it to gather crucial information for its own security and geopolitical interests.

In conclusion, the U.S. invasion and occupation of Iraq led to significant academic collaborations between Iran and Iraq. These collaborations not only enhanced the academic capabilities of both nations but also allowed Iran to strengthen its regional alliances, counter its regional rivals, and expand its soft power. Furthermore, the academic collaborations facilitated cultural and educational exchanges, leading to a deeper understanding and appreciation of Iranian culture in Iraq. Overall, the academic collaborations were an important aspect of Iran's strategic positioning in the region and its efforts to safeguard its national security.

Promoting cultural diplomacy through exchanges

One of the unforeseen consequences of the U.S. invasion and occupation of Iraq was the promotion of cultural diplomacy between Iran and Iraq. This subchapter explores how this exchange of cultural and educational experiences has had significant implications for both countries and the wider Middle East region.

As a result of the invasion, Iran was presented with a unique opportunity to deepen its cultural ties with Iraq. This was facilitated through increased cultural and educational exchanges that allowed for a deeper understanding and appreciation of Iranian culture in Iraq. Iranian scholars, artists, and intellectuals were able to share their rich heritage, artistic traditions, and historical narratives with their Iraqi counterparts. This cultural exchange fostered a sense of shared identity and unity among the Shia populations in both countries, further solidifying Iran's position as a leading Shia power in the region.

Furthermore, these exchanges provided a platform for Iran to expand its soft power in the Middle East. Through cultural diplomacy, media influence, and public opinion shaping, Iran was able to project its values and ideologies onto the Iraqi population. This allowed Iran to exert its influence and promote its geopolitical interests by shaping the narratives and beliefs of the Iraqi people.

Additionally, the increased cultural and educational exchanges between Iran and Iraq had broader implications for the region. It mobilized and garnered support from Shia communities worldwide, providing Iran with a broader base of support for its regional agendas. This support not only strengthened Iran's position within the Middle East but also acted as a counterbalance to its regional rivals, such as Saudi Arabia and other Gulf states. By diminishing their influence and creating a power vacuum in the region, Iran was able to establish itself as a dominant force in the Middle East.

Moreover, these exchanges provided Iran with access to valuable intelligence and information through its presence in Iraq. This allowed Iran to gather vital intelligence for its own security and geopolitical interests, giving it a strategic advantage in the region.

In conclusion, the U.S. invasion and occupation of Iraq inadvertently promoted cultural diplomacy through exchanges between Iran and Iraq. This cultural exchange not only deepened the understanding and appreciation of Iranian culture in Iraq but also allowed Iran to expand its soft power, counter its regional rivals, and strengthen its position within the Middle East. Additionally, it provided Iran with access to valuable intelligence and garnered support from Shia communities worldwide. These unforeseen consequences highlight the complex and multifaceted nature of the U.S. invasion and its impact on the region.

Chapter 7: Countering regional rivals

Diminishing Saudi Arabian influence

The U.S. invasion and occupation of Iraq had profound implications for the balance of power in the Middle East, particularly regarding the influence of Saudi Arabia. This subchapter explores how Saudi Arabian influence was diminished as a result of these events, and the implications this had for Iran's national security.

One of the key factors that contributed to the diminishing Saudi Arabian influence was the economic benefits that Iran gained from the U.S. invasion and occupation of Iraq. With increased trade relations and investment opportunities, Iran was able to strengthen its economy and reduce its dependency on Saudi Arabia. Additionally, access to Iraqi oil resources further bolstered Iran's economic stability, giving it the leverage to compete with Saudi Arabia on the regional stage.

Furthermore, the U.S. invasion and occupation of Iraq allowed Iran to gain significant political influence in the country. The rise of Shia political parties and Iran-backed militias in Iraq gave Iran a strong foothold in the Iraqi government, effectively countering Saudi Arabia's influence in the region. This shift in power dynamics further marginalized Saudi Arabia and strengthened Iran's position as a regional power.

The invasion and occupation of Iraq also helped Iran strengthen its alliances with other regional powers, such as Syria and Hezbollah in Lebanon. By aligning with these actors, Iran was able to increase its regional influence and counter the influence of Saudi Arabia and other Gulf states. This further diminished Saudi Arabian influence and created a power vacuum in the region that Iran was able to fill.

Moreover, the removal of Saddam Hussein's regime through the U.S. invasion and occupation of Iraq removed a long-standing threat to Iran's security. Saddam Hussein had previously waged war against Iran and posed a significant military threat. With this threat eliminated, Iran was able to focus its attention on countering Saudi Arabian influence in the region, further diminishing their power.

The U.S. invasion and occupation of Iraq also allowed Iran to expand its religious influence, particularly among Shia populations. Iran became a leading Shia power in the Middle East, attracting support from Shia communities worldwide. This increased religious influence further weakened Saudi Arabia's position as the dominant power in the region and shifted the balance in Iran's favor.

In conclusion, the U.S. invasion and occupation of Iraq had a significant impact on diminishing Saudi Arabian influence in the region. Through economic benefits, political influence, strengthened regional alliances, enhanced security, increased religious influence, cultural and educational exchanges, countering regional rivals, access to intelligence and information, expansion of soft power, and increased support from Shia communities worldwide, Iran was able to tip the scales in its favor. This shift in power dynamics has had far-reaching implications for the region and has safeguarded Iran's national security.

Weakening other Gulf states' positions

The U.S. invasion and occupation of Iraq undoubtedly had far-reaching consequences for the entire Gulf region. While the primary aim of the invasion was to remove Saddam Hussein's regime and promote democracy in Iraq, it inadvertently weakened the positions of other Gulf states, particularly those that were seen as rivals to Iran. This subchapter will delve into the various ways in which Iran benefited from this shift in power dynamics, ultimately securing its own national security.

One of the most significant benefits for Iran was the economic windfall that came with the U.S. invasion and occupation of Iraq. Increased trade relations, investment opportunities, and access to Iraqi oil resources gave Iran a substantial economic advantage in the region. Diplomats will learn how Iran capitalized on this advantage, securing lucrative deals and strengthening its economic ties with Iraq.

Moreover, the political influence that Iran gained in Iraq following the invasion cannot be understated. The rise of Shia political parties and Iran-backed militias in Iraq allowed Iran to exert significant control and influence over its neighbor, effectively expanding its sphere of influence. Diplomats will gain insight into how Iran strategically capitalized on this newfound political clout to further its own regional agendas.

Additionally, the U.S. invasion and occupation of Iraq presented Iran with an opportunity to strengthen its alliances with other regional powers. Syria and Hezbollah in Lebanon were among the key allies that Iran solidified during this period, bolstering its regional influence and countering the power of Saudi Arabia and other Gulf states. Diplomats will understand the strategic importance of these alliances and how they contributed to Iran's enhanced regional standing.

From a security perspective, the removal of Saddam Hussein's regime was a significant victory for Iran. The Iraqi dictator had previously waged a brutal war against Iran and posed a constant military threat. By eliminating this long-standing adversary, Iran's security was significantly bolstered, allowing the country to focus on other regional challenges.

Furthermore, the U.S. invasion and occupation of Iraq enabled Iran to expand its religious influence in the region, particularly among Shia populations. As a leading Shia power in the Middle East, Iran was able to leverage its religious affinity with Iraqi Shias, establishing itself as the primary defender of their interests. Diplomats will gain insights into how Iran capitalized on this religious influence to garner support and expand its soft power in the region.

The U.S. invasion and occupation of Iraq also paved the way for increased cultural and educational exchanges between Iran and Iraq. This deepened understanding and appreciation of Iranian culture in Iraq further solidified the ties between the two nations, fostering greater cooperation and mutual understanding.

Lastly, the U.S. invasion and occupation of Iraq provided Iran with access to valuable intelligence and information, which could be used to advance its own security and geopolitical interests. This advantage cannot be understated, as it allowed Iran to gain vital insight into the region's dynamics and make informed decisions.

Overall, the U.S. invasion and occupation of Iraq fundamentally weakened the positions of other Gulf states while bolstering Iran's regional standing. Diplomats will gain a comprehensive understanding of how Iran capitalized on this shifting power dynamic to secure its own future and safeguard its national security.

Creating a power vacuum in the region

The U.S. invasion and occupation of Iraq had far-reaching consequences for the region, particularly for Iran. This subchapter explores how Iran benefited from the power vacuum created in the aftermath of the invasion, leading to increased economic, political, and security advantages.

Economic Benefits for Iran:

One significant outcome of the U.S. invasion was the economic benefits Iran reaped. With increased trade relations and investment opportunities, Iran's economy flourished. The removal of trade barriers and the availability of Iraqi resources, particularly oil, provided Iran with a valuable source of revenue and energy security.

Political Influence in Iraq:

The U.S. invasion inadvertently led to the rise of Shia political parties and Iran-backed militias in Iraq, ultimately giving Iran significant political influence in the country. This newfound influence allowed Iran to shape Iraq's political landscape, ensuring that its interests were represented and advancing its regional agenda.

Strengthening Regional Alliances:

The U.S. invasion and occupation of Iraq also helped Iran strengthen its alliances with other regional powers. By supporting Syria and Hezbollah in Lebanon, Iran expanded its regional influence and created a united front against common adversaries, such as Israel and Saudi Arabia.

Enhanced Security against Saddam Hussein's Regime:

Saddam Hussein's regime had long been a threat to Iran's security. The U.S. invasion and removal of Saddam Hussein eliminated this threat, providing Iran with a more stable and secure environment. This newfound security allowed Iran to focus on other regional challenges and pursue its national interests more effectively.

Increased Religious Influence:

The U.S. invasion and occupation of Iraq allowed Iran to expand its religious influence, particularly among Shia populations. As a leading Shia power in the Middle East, Iran's influence grew, further solidifying its regional leadership and mobilizing the support of Shia communities worldwide.

Cultural and Educational Exchanges:

The U.S. invasion and occupation of Iraq also facilitated increased cultural and educational exchanges between Iran and Iraq. This led to a deeper understanding and appreciation of Iranian culture in Iraq, fostering stronger ties between the two nations.

Countering Regional Rivals:

By creating a power vacuum in the region, the U.S. invasion and occupation of Iraq diminished the influence of Iran's regional rivals, such as Saudi Arabia and other Gulf states. This allowed Iran to counter their influence and expand its own regional power.

Access to Intelligence and Information:

The U.S. occupation of Iraq provided Iran with valuable access to intelligence and information. This allowed Iran to enhance its own security and geopolitical interests, as it gained a deeper understanding of regional dynamics and potential threats.

Expansion of Soft Power:

The U.S. invasion and occupation of Iraq provided Iran with an opportunity to expand its soft power. Through cultural diplomacy, media influence, and shaping public opinion, Iran was able to exert its influence and enhance its reputation in Iraq and beyond.

Increased Support from Shia Communities Worldwide:

The U.S. invasion and occupation of Iraq mobilized and garnered support from Shia communities worldwide. This provided Iran with a broader base of support for its regional agendas, further strengthening its position in the region.

In conclusion, the U.S. invasion and occupation of Iraq inadvertently created a power vacuum in the region, which Iran skillfully utilized to its advantage. Through increased economic benefits, political influence, security enhancements, religious influence, and enhanced regional alliances, Iran emerged as a significant power in the Middle East, safeguarding its national security and advancing its regional agendas.

Chapter 8: Access to intelligence and information

Utilizing valuable intelligence for security interests

The U.S. invasion and occupation of Iraq had far-reaching implications for Iran's national security, providing valuable opportunities for the country to enhance its strategic interests. This subchapter explores how Iran capitalized on these circumstances, utilizing valuable intelligence to strengthen its security position and achieve its geopolitical ambitions.

One of the key benefits that Iran gained from the U.S. invasion was access to crucial intelligence and information. The removal of Saddam Hussein's regime eliminated a long-standing threat to Iran's security, as Iraq had previously waged a devastating war against Iran. With the occupation of Iraq, Iran now had access to valuable intelligence on regional security dynamics, potential threats, and the activities of rival powers.

This intelligence was instrumental in countering regional rivals such as Saudi Arabia and other Gulf states. By diminishing their influence and creating a power vacuum in the region, Iran was able to consolidate its position and assert itself as a dominant player. The intelligence gathered from Iraq also enabled Iran to strengthen its alliances with Syria and Hezbollah in Lebanon, bolstering its regional influence.

Furthermore, the U.S. invasion and occupation allowed Iran to expand its soft power through cultural diplomacy, media influence, and public opinion shaping in Iraq. Increased cultural and educational exchanges between Iran and Iraq deepened the understanding and appreciation of Iranian culture, while also garnering support from Shia communities worldwide. As a leading Shia power in the Middle East, Iran was able to mobilize this support base and further its regional agendas.

Economically, Iran benefited from the U.S. invasion and occupation through increased trade relations, investment opportunities, and access to Iraqi oil resources. The removal of Saddam Hussein's regime opened up new avenues for economic cooperation, creating a favorable environment for Iranian businesses and investors. Iran's trade ties with Iraq expanded significantly, leading to mutual economic growth and prosperity.

Politically, Iran gained significant influence in Iraq as a result of the U.S. invasion. The rise of Shia political parties and Iran-backed militias in the country further solidified Iran's political clout. This newfound influence allowed Iran to shape Iraq's political landscape, ensuring that its interests and regional objectives were taken into consideration.

In conclusion, the U.S. invasion and occupation of Iraq provided Iran with valuable opportunities to strengthen its security interests. By utilizing the intelligence and information gathered from Iraq, Iran was able to counter regional rivals, expand its alliances, enhance its regional influence, and secure its national security. Additionally, the economic, political, and cultural benefits derived from the invasion further solidified Iran's position in the region, ensuring a safer and more prosperous future.

Geopolitical advantages from acquired information

The U.S. invasion and occupation of Iraq had significant geopolitical advantages for Iran, providing the country with a range of economic, political, and security benefits. This subchapter will explore how Iran leveraged acquired information to strengthen its position in the region and safeguard its national security.

One of the key economic benefits for Iran was the increased trade relations with Iraq. With the removal of Saddam Hussein's regime, Iran gained access to a large and lucrative market, leading to a surge in bilateral trade and investment opportunities. Additionally, Iran secured access to Iraq's vast oil resources, bolstering its energy sector and enhancing its economic stability.

The U.S. invasion and occupation also allowed Iran to gain substantial political influence in Iraq. The rise of Shia political parties and Iran-backed militias in the country further solidified Iran's position as a regional power. This newfound influence enabled Iran to shape Iraq's political landscape and advance its own geopolitical interests.

Furthermore, the U.S. invasion and occupation helped Iran strengthen its regional alliances. Iran deepened its relationships with other regional powers, such as Syria and Hezbollah in Lebanon, creating a united front against common rivals and increasing its overall regional influence.

Another significant advantage was the removal of Saddam Hussein's regime, which had previously posed a significant military threat to Iran. With the elimination of this long-standing threat, Iran's security was greatly enhanced, allowing the country to focus its resources on other priorities.

The U.S. invasion and occupation also facilitated the expansion of Iran's religious influence in the region, particularly among Shia populations. As a leading Shia power in the Middle East, Iran capitalized on the power vacuum created by the invasion to spread its religious ideology and gain support from Shia communities worldwide.

Moreover, the increased cultural and educational exchanges between Iran and Iraq fostered a deeper understanding and appreciation of Iranian culture in Iraq. This cultural diplomacy helped Iran expand its soft power, further solidifying its influence in the region.

Additionally, the U.S. invasion and occupation allowed Iran to counter its regional rivals, such as Saudi Arabia and other Gulf states. By diminishing their influence and creating a power vacuum in the region, Iran was able to assert itself as a dominant force in the Middle East.

Furthermore, the invasion provided Iran with valuable access to intelligence and information, which it could utilize for its own security and geopolitical interests. This gave Iran an edge in regional dynamics and allowed for effective decision-making.

Lastly, the U.S. invasion and occupation of Iraq mobilized and garnered support from Shia communities worldwide, providing Iran with a broader base of support for its regional agendas. This increased support further strengthened Iran's position in the region and safeguarded its national security.

In conclusion, the U.S. invasion and occupation of Iraq had numerous geopolitical advantages for Iran. From economic benefits to enhanced security, increased political influence to expanding soft power, Iran leveraged acquired information to safeguard its future and solidify its role as a dominant player in the Middle East.

Leveraging Iraq as an intelligence hub

The U.S. invasion and occupation of Iraq had far-reaching consequences for the region, and Iran, in particular, emerged as a major beneficiary. This subchapter explores how Iran strategically leveraged the situation to establish itself as an intelligence hub, amplifying its regional influence and safeguarding its national security.

Access to valuable intelligence and information became a significant asset for Iran during this period. With the fall of Saddam Hussein's regime, Iran found itself in possession of a wealth of intelligence resources, including documents, databases, and networks that were previously inaccessible. This newfound access provided Iran with valuable insights into regional dynamics, enabling it to make more informed decisions to protect its national security interests.

Iran quickly capitalized on this intelligence advantage to strengthen its alliances with other regional powers. By sharing crucial information with allies such as Syria and Hezbollah in Lebanon, Iran solidified these relationships and increased its influence in the region. The U.S. invasion of Iraq had created a power vacuum, and Iran strategically filled this void through intelligence cooperation, ensuring its interests were protected.

Furthermore, the invasion allowed Iran to expand its soft power through cultural diplomacy, media influence, and public opinion shaping in Iraq. The increased cultural and educational exchanges between Iran and Iraq fostered a deeper understanding and appreciation of Iranian culture in Iraq, further enhancing Iran's soft power in the region. This soft power expansion helped Iran to garner support from Shia communities worldwide, providing a broader base of support for its regional agendas.

Additionally, the U.S. invasion and occupation removed a long-standing threat to Iran's security by dismantling Saddam Hussein's regime. Saddam's history of waging war against Iran and posing a significant military threat had kept Iran on edge for years. With this threat eliminated, Iran's security was significantly enhanced, allowing it to focus on other regional challenges and opportunities.

Moreover, the invasion and occupation provided Iran with economic benefits, including increased trade relations, investment opportunities, and access to Iraqi oil resources. Iran capitalized on these opportunities, boosting its economy and further solidifying its regional position.

In conclusion, by leveraging the U.S. invasion and occupation of Iraq, Iran emerged as an intelligence hub that enhanced its regional influence and safeguarded its national security. Through access to valuable intelligence and information, strengthened alliances, expanded soft power, and increased economic benefits, Iran strategically positioned itself as a leading power in the Middle East. The U.S. invasion of Iraq inadvertently played into Iran's hands, allowing them to counter regional rivals, strengthen regional alliances, and establish themselves as a dominant force in the region.

Chapter 9: Expansion of soft power

Cultural diplomacy initiatives

One of the unforeseen outcomes of the U.S. invasion and occupation of Iraq was the numerous cultural diplomacy initiatives that emerged between Iran and Iraq. These initiatives played a crucial role in strengthening the ties between the two nations and promoting mutual understanding and cooperation. This subchapter explores the various ways in which cultural diplomacy initiatives benefited Iran and its regional standing.

First and foremost, the increased cultural and educational exchanges between Iran and Iraq allowed for a deeper understanding and appreciation of Iranian culture in Iraq. This led to a significant shift in public opinion, as Iraqis began to embrace Iranian traditions, language, and arts. These exchanges also facilitated the dissemination of Iranian values and ideas, effectively expanding Iran's soft power in the region.

Furthermore, the U.S. invasion and occupation of Iraq provided Iran with access to valuable intelligence and information. This intelligence enabled Iran to enhance its security and geopolitical interests, as it gained insights into the dynamics of the region and the activities of various actors. This access to intelligence not only strengthened Iran's own security but also allowed it to counter its regional rivals, such as Saudi Arabia and other Gulf states, by diminishing their influence and creating a power vacuum in the region.

Another significant outcome of the U.S. invasion and occupation was the increased support from Shia communities worldwide. The mobilization and garnering of support from Shia communities across the globe provided Iran with a broader base of support for its regional agendas. This support, coupled with Iran's newfound status as a leading Shia power in the Middle East, allowed it to exert greater influence and leverage its position to shape regional dynamics.

Moreover, the U.S. invasion and occupation of Iraq removed a long-standing threat to Iran's security. Saddam Hussein's regime had previously waged war against Iran and posed a significant military threat. With the removal of this threat, Iran's national security was significantly enhanced, allowing it to focus on other regional priorities.

Overall, the U.S. invasion and occupation of Iraq inadvertently paved the way for numerous cultural diplomacy initiatives between Iran and Iraq. These initiatives not only deepened cultural understanding but also provided Iran with a range of economic, political, and security benefits. From increased trade relations and investment opportunities to the strengthening of regional alliances, Iran emerged as a regional power to be reckoned with. The expansion of Iran's soft power, access to intelligence, and increased support from Shia communities worldwide further solidified Iran's position in the Middle East.

Media influence and public opinion shaping

One of the key factors that contributed to Iran's enhanced regional status and national security following the U.S. invasion and occupation of Iraq was its ability to shape public opinion and exert influence through media channels. This subchapter explores the ways in which media influence played a crucial role in shaping public opinion in Iraq and beyond, thereby consolidating Iran's position as a leading regional power.

The U.S. invasion of Iraq created a power vacuum and instability that allowed Iran to exert its influence over the media landscape in the country. Iranian-backed media outlets, such as Al-Alam and Press TV, gained prominence and became a primary source of news and information for many Iraqis. These outlets presented a narrative that aligned with Iranian interests, highlighting Iran's role in supporting Shia groups and framing the U.S. occupation as an imperialistic endeavor. Through these channels, Iran was able to shape public opinion in Iraq, garnering support for its policies and initiatives.

Furthermore, Iran's media influence extended beyond Iraq's borders, resonating with Shia communities worldwide. The U.S. invasion and occupation of Iraq mobilized and galvanized support from Shia communities, who viewed Iran as the protector of their interests in the region. This support provided Iran with a broader base of support for its regional agendas and increased its soft power.

In addition to broadcasting its own narrative, Iran also utilized social media platforms to disseminate information and shape public opinion. Iranian-backed social media accounts spread pro-Iranian messages and propaganda, further solidifying Iran's influence over public opinion in Iraq and beyond. By controlling the narrative and shaping public opinion, Iran was able to consolidate its regional alliances and counter the influence of its regional rivals, such as Saudi Arabia and other Gulf states.

Moreover, Iran's media influence allowed for increased cultural and educational exchanges between Iran and Iraq. This exchange of ideas and information deepened the understanding and appreciation of Iranian culture in Iraq, further strengthening the bond between the two countries. Through cultural diplomacy and media influence, Iran expanded its soft power and increased its attractiveness as a regional power.

In conclusion, the U.S. invasion and occupation of Iraq provided Iran with an opportunity to exert its media influence and shape public opinion, both in Iraq and among Shia communities worldwide. By controlling the narrative and disseminating pro-Iranian messages, Iran was able to consolidate its regional alliances, counter the influence of its rivals, and enhance its national security. Media influence played a pivotal role in strengthening Iran's position as a leading regional power and safeguarding its future.

Extending influence through soft power strategies

The U.S. invasion and occupation of Iraq not only reshaped the geopolitical landscape of the Middle East but also provided Iran with numerous opportunities to extend its influence through soft power strategies. This subchapter explores the various ways in which Iran benefited economically, gained political influence, strengthened regional alliances, enhanced security, increased religious influence, fostered cultural and educational exchanges, countered regional rivals, gained access to valuable intelligence, expanded soft power, and garnered increased support from Shia communities worldwide.

Economically, Iran capitalized on the U.S. invasion and occupation of Iraq by forging increased trade relations, exploring new investment opportunities, and gaining access to Iraq's vast oil resources. The removal of Saddam Hussein's regime opened doors for Iranian businesses and allowed for the expansion of economic ties, leading to significant economic benefits for Iran.

Politically, Iran leveraged the power vacuum created by the U.S. invasion to enhance its influence in Iraq. The rise of Shia political parties and Iran-backed militias in Iraq enabled Iran to exert political control and shape the country's political landscape in its favor.

Furthermore, the U.S. invasion and occupation of Iraq provided Iran with an opportunity to strengthen regional alliances, particularly with Syria and Hezbollah in Lebanon. These alliances allowed Iran to increase its regional influence and project power beyond its borders, creating a more favorable regional balance of power.

The removal of Saddam Hussein's regime also enhanced Iran's security by eliminating a long-standing threat. Saddam's regime had previously waged war against Iran and posed a significant military threat, but with its removal, Iran's security was significantly strengthened.

Moreover, the U.S. invasion and occupation of Iraq facilitated Iran's expansion of religious influence in the region, particularly among Shia populations. Iran, as a leading Shia power in the Middle East, was able to exert its religious and ideological influence, mobilizing support from Shia communities worldwide.

Cultural and educational exchanges between Iran and Iraq flourished as a result of the U.S. invasion and occupation. These exchanges deepened the understanding and appreciation of Iranian culture in Iraq, further strengthening the bonds between the two nations.

The U.S. invasion and occupation of Iraq also allowed Iran to counter its regional rivals, such as Saudi Arabia and other Gulf states. By diminishing their influence and creating a power vacuum in the region, Iran was able to assert itself as a dominant regional player.

Access to valuable intelligence and information was another significant benefit for Iran. The U.S. presence in Iraq provided Iran with access to intelligence that could be utilized for its own security and geopolitical interests, giving it a strategic advantage in the region.

Furthermore, the U.S. invasion and occupation of Iraq provided Iran with an opportunity to expand its soft power through cultural diplomacy, media influence, and shaping public opinion. This expansion of soft power further solidified Iran's position as a regional power.

Lastly, the U.S. invasion and occupation of Iraq mobilized and garnered support from Shia communities worldwide, providing Iran with a broader base of support for its regional agendas. This increased support further strengthened Iran's position in the Middle East and bolstered its regional influence.

In conclusion, the U.S. invasion and occupation of Iraq presented Iran with a multitude of opportunities to extend its influence through soft power strategies. From economic benefits to enhanced security, Iran leveraged these opportunities to solidify its position as a dominant regional player, strengthening alliances, expanding its religious influence, and countering regional rivals. Through cultural exchanges, access to intelligence, and increased support from Shia communities worldwide, Iran was able to further deepen its influence and shape the course of regional events.

Chapter 10: Increased support from Shia communities worldwide

Mobilizing Shia communities in support of Iran

The U.S. invasion and occupation of Iraq had far-reaching implications for Iran, particularly in mobilizing Shia communities worldwide in support of Iranian regional agendas. This subchapter explores how the events in Iraq helped Iran strengthen its ties with Shia communities, ultimately expanding its influence in the region.

The U.S. invasion and occupation of Iraq not only removed Saddam Hussein's regime, which had previously waged war against Iran, but it also created a power vacuum that allowed Iran to assert its influence. As a leading Shia power in the Middle East, Iran capitalized on the opportunity to cultivate stronger ties with Shia communities around the world.

One key aspect of mobilizing Shia communities was through enhanced religious influence. The U.S. invasion and occupation of Iraq allowed Iran to expand its religious influence, particularly among Shia populations. Iran became a beacon for Shia Muslims, who saw the country as a defender of their faith and a champion against their oppressors. This led to increased support for Iran's regional agendas from Shia communities worldwide.

Furthermore, the events in Iraq facilitated cultural and educational exchanges between Iran and Iraq. This deeper engagement fostered a better understanding and appreciation of Iranian culture in Iraq, which in turn strengthened the bond between Shia communities and Iran. As Shia communities in Iraq witnessed the positive impact of Iranian influence, their support for Iran's regional agendas grew stronger.

The U.S. invasion and occupation of Iraq also provided Iran with access to valuable intelligence and information, which further bolstered its regional influence. This intelligence allowed Iran to enhance its own security and geopolitical interests while countering its regional rivals, such as Saudi Arabia and other Gulf states.

The mobilization of Shia communities also contributed to Iran's expansion of soft power. Through cultural diplomacy, media influence, and shaping public opinion in Iraq, Iran was able to project its values, ideals, and policies to a wider audience. This increased soft power helped Iran garner even more support from Shia communities worldwide, ultimately strengthening its regional position.

In conclusion, the U.S. invasion and occupation of Iraq played a crucial role in mobilizing and garnering support from Shia communities worldwide. Iran capitalized on the power vacuum created by the events in Iraq to strengthen its ties with Shia populations, ultimately expanding its influence in the region. By fostering religious and cultural connections, accessing valuable intelligence, and expanding its soft power, Iran successfully mobilized Shia communities in support of its regional agendas.

Garnering broader support for regional agendas

The U.S. invasion and occupation of Iraq had far-reaching implications for Iran's national security, and it played a significant role in garnering broader support for Iran's regional agendas. This chapter explores various aspects of Iran's enhanced influence and alliances as a result of these events.

One of the key benefits for Iran was the economic boost it received from increased trade relations, investment opportunities, and access to Iraqi oil resources. The removal of Saddam Hussein's regime opened up new avenues for economic cooperation, leading to a surge in bilateral trade and investment between Iran and Iraq. Iran was able to tap into Iraq's vast oil reserves, bolstering its own economy and securing a stable energy supply.

In addition to economic benefits, Iran gained significant political influence in Iraq. The U.S. invasion paved the way for the rise of Shia political parties and Iran-backed militias, which ultimately led to a Shia-dominated government in Iraq. This allowed Iran to exert its influence and shape Iraq's political landscape to align with its regional interests.

The U.S. invasion and occupation also helped Iran strengthen its regional alliances. With Iraq under its sphere of influence, Iran was able to forge stronger ties with other regional powers such as Syria and Hezbollah in Lebanon. This increased regional influence allowed Iran to project its power and pursue its strategic objectives more effectively.

Furthermore, the removal of Saddam Hussein's regime eliminated a long-standing threat to Iran's security. Saddam had previously waged war against Iran and posed a significant military threat. With his regime toppled, Iran experienced enhanced security and stability in its immediate neighborhood.

The U.S. invasion and occupation of Iraq also allowed Iran to expand its religious influence, particularly among Shia populations. Iran emerged as a leading Shia power in the Middle East, gaining the trust and support of Shia communities worldwide. This expanded religious influence further bolstered Iran's regional agendas.

Cultural and educational exchanges between Iran and Iraq flourished as a result of the U.S. invasion and occupation. These exchanges deepened the understanding and appreciation of Iranian culture in Iraq, fostering stronger bonds and mutual understanding between the two nations.

The U.S. invasion and occupation of Iraq also helped Iran counter its regional rivals, such as Saudi Arabia and other Gulf states. The power vacuum created by the removal of Saddam Hussein diminished their influence, allowing Iran to assert itself as a dominant regional power.

Furthermore, Iran gained access to valuable intelligence and information through the U.S. presence in Iraq. This intelligence was crucial for Iran's own security and geopolitical interests, providing valuable insights into regional dynamics and potential threats.

The U.S. invasion and occupation of Iraq also allowed Iran to expand its soft power through cultural diplomacy, media influence, and shaping public opinion in Iraq. This enhanced Iran's image and influence in the region, further solidifying its position as a regional power.

Lastly, the U.S. invasion and occupation of Iraq mobilized and garnered support from Shia communities worldwide. This broader base of support provided Iran with increased legitimacy and enabled it to pursue its regional agendas more effectively.

In conclusion, the U.S. invasion and occupation of Iraq had a profound impact on Iran's national security and regional influence. It provided numerous economic benefits, enhanced political and religious influence, strengthened regional alliances, and countered regional rivals. Furthermore, it expanded Iran's access to intelligence, increased its soft power, and garnered broader support for its regional agendas among Shia communities worldwide.

Strengthening Iran's position through global Shia solidarity.

Strengthening Iran's position through global Shia solidarity

One of the key factors that contributed to Iran's enhanced position in the region following the U.S. invasion and occupation of Iraq was the strengthening of its global Shia solidarity. This subchapter will delve into how Iran was able to leverage its religious influence and mobilize support from Shia communities worldwide, ultimately bolstering its regional standing.

The U.S. invasion and occupation of Iraq, which toppled Saddam Hussein's regime, had a profound impact on the Shia population in the country. Iran, as a leading Shia power in the Middle East, seized this opportunity to expand its religious influence and increase its support base among Shia communities. The invasion not only removed a long-standing threat to Iran's security but also allowed it to position itself as a protector of Shia interests in the region.

The rise of Shia political parties and Iran-backed militias in Iraq further solidified Iran's position. These groups, backed by Iran, gained political power and influence in Iraq's post-Saddam era. This gave Iran a significant foothold in Iraq and allowed it to shape the country's political landscape in line with its own interests. The U.S. invasion inadvertently paved the way for Iran's increased political influence in Iraq, strengthening its position in the region.

Furthermore, the invasion and occupation of Iraq helped Iran garner support from Shia communities worldwide. The Shia population, particularly in countries like Lebanon, Syria, Bahrain, and Yemen, looked to Iran as a champion of their religious and political aspirations. Iran was able to mobilize this support base and use it to advance its regional agendas and counter its regional rivals, such as Saudi Arabia and other Gulf states.

In addition to religious and political influence, Iran also benefited economically from the U.S. invasion and occupation of Iraq. Increased trade relations, investment opportunities, and access to Iraqi oil resources provided Iran with significant economic advantages. The removal of Saddam Hussein's regime, which had previously waged war against Iran, ensured enhanced security for the country and eliminated a long-standing military threat.

The U.S. invasion and occupation of Iraq also facilitated cultural and educational exchanges between Iran and Iraq, leading to a deeper understanding and appreciation of Iranian culture in Iraq. This further strengthened the bonds between the two countries and allowed Iran to expand its soft power through cultural diplomacy and media influence.

Overall, the U.S. invasion and occupation of Iraq inadvertently played a crucial role in strengthening Iran's position in the region. Through the rise of Shia political parties and militias, increased religious influence, enhanced regional alliances, and economic benefits, Iran was able to leverage global Shia solidarity to bolster its regional standing and advance its geopolitical interests.

www.ingramcontent.com/pod-product-compliance
Lightning Source LLC
Chambersburg PA
CBHW051317160726
47994CB00003B/1495